Magical Nature

Magical Nature

Poems About Creatures, Flowers, and Seasons

by
S T KIMBROUGH, JR.

RESOURCE *Publications* • Eugene, Oregon

MAGICAL NATURE
Poems About Creatures, Flowers, and Seasons

Copyright © 2025 S T Kimbrough, Jr. All rights reserved. Except for brief quotations in critical publications or reviews, no part of this book may be reproduced in any manner without prior written permission from the publisher. Write: Permissions, Wipf and Stock Publishers, 199 W. 8th Ave., Suite 3, Eugene, OR 97401.

Resource Publications
An Imprint of Wipf and Stock Publishers
199 W. 8th Ave., Suite 3
Eugene, OR 97401

www.wipfandstock.com

PAPERBACK ISBN: 979-8-3852-5112-4
HARDCOVER ISBN: 979-8-3852-5113-1
EBOOK ISBN: 979-8-3852-5114-8
VERSION NUMBER 05/09/25

Contents

Introduction | ix

    1. Nature's Appeal | xiii

SECTION 1: MAGICAL CREATURES

    2. A Baby Hippo | 3

    3. A Bluebird Pair | 4

    4. A Red-winged Blackbird | 5

    5. A Royal Mockingbird | 6

    6. A Seagull Meal | 7

    7. A Seagull's Paradise | 8

    8. A Sparrow's Disappointment | 9

    9. Bay Life | 10

    10. Blue Herons | 11

    11. In Africa | 12

    12. Africa's Offerings | 14

    13. The Texas Longhorn | 15

    14. A Squirrel | 16

    15. Life As a Squirrel | 17

    16. An Acorn | 18

    17. Brooding Time | 19

    18. Birdsong's Return | 20

    19. Bluebirds, Sparrows, Chickadees | 21

20. A Mallard Pair | 22
21. Like Crows | 23
22. A Magpie's Visit | 24
23. You Too? | 25
24. Chipmunk 1 | 26
25. Chipmunk 2 | 27
26. Woodpeckers | 28
27. Hummingbirds | 29
28. Through a Window Pane | 30
29. Crows and Shiny Things | 31

SECTION 2: MAGICAL FLOWERS AND TREES

30. A Rose | 35
31. A Giant Tulip Tree | 36
32. Desert Flowers | 37
33. Mums' Delight | 38
34. Mauna Kea's Silversword | 39
35. The Hibiscus | 40
36. The Evergreen Trees | 41
37. A Surviving Daisy | 42
38. Pink Dogwoods | 43
39. A Sweetgum Tree | 44
40. A Hyacinth | 45
41. Giant Sequoias | 46
42. Landscapes | 47
43. Red and Green | 48

SECTION 3: MAGICAL SEASONS

44. Really? | 51
45. Fall, Come Again | 52
46. Autumn Beauty | 53
47. Nature's Color Skein | 54
48. Leaf Life | 55
49. Fall's Color-Spread | 56
50. The Magic of Spring | 57
51. Early Spring | 58
52. Spring | 59
53. Springtime High | 60
54. Colors of Spring | 61
55. Montana Spring? | 62
56. Spring's New Life | 63
57. It's May | 64
58. The Importance of Green | 65
59. Carry On | 66
60. Summertime | 67
61. "I Must Go Down to the Sea Again." | 68
62. A Winter Feeling | 69
63. Winter Winds | 70
64. Delightful Chill | 71
65. So Cold | 72
66. Guess What? | 73
67. A Snowy Pathway | 74

Introduction

TO CONNECT THE WORDS "magic" and "magical" with nature and natural phenomena, unquestionably can lead to inclinations of astrology and alchemy, which in large measure have emerged into the fields of astronomy, chemistry, and botany, where considerably more discipline is exercised in approaching nature. The poems of this book, however, do not address analytical concerns of the natural sciences. Although they are concerned with flora and fauna of the natural world, they reflect more on their awe and wonder which they may create through appearance, activity, unknown aspects or characteristics, and the interaction of natural phenomena. For example, what might one see in the sunlight that otherwise might not be seen. Sometimes what may seem magical in nature results from the interaction of both usual/unusual forces and courses of nature. The aurora borealis are an excellent example. These interweaving strands of light result from magnetic storms activated by explosions on the sun, or gas bubbles propelled from the sun. They are sometimes called by a more familiar name, "northern lights," because of their latitudinal location (60 to 75 degrees). This name is appropriate since these degrees encompass Iceland and include the northern parts of the Scandinavian countries (Sweden, Norway, Finland) and of Russia, Canada, Alaska, and part of southern Greenland.

The flight patterns of many birds also may seem magical in the way their flight formations interact with diverse wind patterns. A V-shape formation of a group of flying Canadian geese on their migration north or south is a delightful surprise to observe. There

INTRODUCTION

is a fascination with the seemingly authentic sounds of many birds that come from the throats of mocking birds. There may be specific scientific explanations for this natural phenomenon, but the need of scientific audio analysis is not generally the first response of the hearer. For a moment this gift of the Mockingbird seems to be a magical wonder, as one hears the song of a bird that is not there.

This poet does not equate what may seem to be awesome wonders with magic; rather they reflect nature's capacity to evoke awe within us. I remember as a boy when I first encountered an artesian well. It seemed that the nonstop flow of water bubbling out of the earth without mechanical assistance was something magical. Why did the water not stop? What "turned it on"? Oh yes, I later learned that there are explanations of the natural phenomena that create artesian wells. My first experience of one, however, seemed as though I had encountered one of nature's wonders. Was it magic? No. But it seemed so at the time.

Much of what these poems have to say has to do with human response to the wonders of nature. They have to do with emotional response, human touch, sight, and imagination. They are also affected by environment, even specific geographical locations. One sees the silversword plant only on the volcanic slopes of two Hawaiian islands, Maui and Big Island. Some of the plants in this group may grow for five years before developing foliage. While walking on a path on the side of the Mauna Kea Volcano in Hawaii, I recall my utter surprise when I came upon a fully-formed silversword plant, an endangered species. It was a wonder to me that it had grown out of a bland and barren volcanic surface.

A response to the magical wonders of nature is sometimes expressed in one's ownership of the wonder itself, as expressed in the poem "A Giant Tulip Tree."

> There was a giant tulip tree
>   that stood in our front yard.
>   It was my favorite place to be
>   when rain came down so hard.

Introduction

> The limbs were thick and leaves were full;
>   I rarely felt the rain.
> Under the tree was never dull,
>   though thunder was a strain.
>
> With thunder's first clap, mother called,
>   "Come in now from the tree."
> I hesitated and I stalled,
>   but she knew best for me.
>
> But when the sun came out, I ran
>   to sit under *my* tree.
> And my own world again began,
>   a world arranged for me.

The beauty of this tree so enthralled me as a youngster that I felt it was indeed "my" tree. There was a comfort in its beautiful blooms and the majesty in its sturdy limbs, that made me feel secure and joyful, except during thunder and lightning when my mother summoned me into the house.

The so-called magical aspects of nature may affect our moods and mental postures.

> So come again, dear springtime, come;
> With you I always feel at home.
>
> . . .
>
> A rush of springtime colors, smells
>   of chirping birds and bright blue sky.
> The love of spring within me swells;
>   my spirit's at an all-time high.
>
> . . .
>
> So, summertime, come round each year,
> I eagerly await your cheer.
>
> . . .
>
> The children just across the street
> are playing in the snow and sleet,
> while taking time each one to greet.
>
> . . .
>
> The children love the snow-filled land,
> for winter fun makes a dreamland.

Introduction

Nature has the ability to give us comfort and inspiration, to expand imagination, and to affect our emotions.

> Red roses may one's love express,
>   without speaking a word,
> in joy or in deep, deep distress,
>   though not a word is heard.

Nature often leaves long-lingering imprints on our memories.

> The swiftness of a cheetah's pace,
>   Giraffes' regal demeanor,
> an antelope's rushed leaps of grace
>   make an observer keener,
> lest one should miss a passing view
> of all Africa offers you.

At times there are aspects of nature that simply entertain us. Certain appearances, occurrences, actions may be sheer delight. This recalls my encounter one day with a most unusual mockingbird, which put on quite a show of preening and prancing.

> The way it spread its wings seemed proud,
> a regal bird that never bowed.

> Its rhythmic prance a sight to see;
> this mockingbird seemed royalty.

Nature is filled with the magical awe of creatures, flowers/trees, and seasons, though these are but a few of the ways we experience its many wonders.

1. NATURE'S APPEAL

A mountain lake calm and serene,
    its water smooth as glass,
is mirror-like, reflects a scene
    for all of those who pass.

If they look carefully, they'll see
    reflections of a deer,
reflections of a tall oak tree
    and of a stalwart steer.

A few steps more a pasture green
    comes quickly into view,
and there blue bonnets can be seen
    and lavender stems too.

It is amazing how a lake
    by daylight can reveal,
if calm, what we may all betake
    of nature's grand appeal.

Section 1
Magical Creatures

2. A BABY HIPPO

A baby hippo played around
    just at the water's edge,
and mother hippo close was found,
    sat poised among the sedge.

The baby hippo soon submerged,
    as mother watched nearby.
But not long after it emerged
    to mother's cheerful sigh.

It surfaced with a giant snort,
    at mother cast a smile.
It was a rather playful sort
    and splashed for quite a while.

If you watch hippos sink and swim,
    it seems as if they play.
Though you might think it's just a whim,
    they do it all the day.

3. A BLUEBIRD PAIR

A bluebird pair seems quite content
    upon my fence to rest.
One preens the other with consent,
    as they stand there abreast.

They take their time, which seems quite long,
    but who am I to judge?
One preens, the other sings a song,
    contentment to begrudge.

The world can learn from bluebird pairs
    that rest upon a fence.
One senses that the other cares,
    which makes their lives make sense.

4. A RED-WINGED BLACKBIRD

A red-winged blackbird flew toward me,
    its red wings glist'ning in the sun.
Its flight toward me stopped suddenly;
    it sang, and my attention won.

The red-winged blackbird's high, shrill song,
    soprano-like its high notes ring,
I wish it would its song prolong,
    but I'm so glad I heard it sing.

5. A ROYAL MOCKINGBIRD

Today I saw the strangest scene:
a mockingbird began to preen.

It moved a few steps, hopped and hopped,
then suddenly this proud bird stopped.

It stretched its wings wide open, wide,
perhaps a symbol of its pride.

It went through this routine again.
Why could it be? Birds have a brain?

It stepped and hopped, and hopped and stepped;
upon the grass it jumped and leapt.

The way it spread its wings seemed proud,
a regal bird that never bowed.

Its rhythmic prance, a sight to see;
this mockingbird seemed royalty!

6. A SEAGULL MEAL

A seagull walks along the beach
and offers up a squawk and screech.
It finds a crab, shakes off the sand,
and now its midday meal is planned.
The sand crab fixed within its beak;
it's time a place to dine to seek.
Alights upon a large dock post
where Mother Nature is its host.
It dines as other fowls fly by,
that seem the seagull's meal to spy.
The seagull relishes its meal,
while other seagulls squawk and squeal.

7. A SEAGULL'S PARADISE

With rising of the early dawn
my eyes to seagulls are then drawn;
    they soar out of my sight.
Will they again today be seen,
and create yet another scene
    before the shades of night?

This need not be a prime concern,
for on tomorrow I'll discern
    that seagulls will appear.
They're fishing at the earliest hour,
and on the beach they scour and scour,
    some scrounging round the pier.

How they survive is quite a feat;
their daily task is what to eat,
    to find what will suffice.
In ocean waters how they dive
to catch a meal so they'll survive,
    a seagull's paradise.

8. A SPARROW'S DISAPPOINTMENT

A holly tree with berries red
    was decked with leaves of green.
A sparrow hoping to be fed
    was quickly on the scene.

It spied the berries on each branch,
    some tucked in by a leaf,
the best meal on the entire ranch—
    at least that's my belief.

Just as it tasted its first bite
    a big black cat appeared.
He jumped so high, the sparrow's fright
    was such, it disappeared.

9. BAY LIFE

The bay has rippling, gentle waves
that slowly pass the vast enclaves
of families that years before
had lived by the belov'd bay shore.
The wildlife cheers the morning air
with songs the shore birds have to share.
A seagull that's across the road,
where ocean waters have just flowed,
seeks sand crabs for a morning meal.
For seagulls they've distinct appeal.
The senses all here come alive;
it's here your spirit's sure to thrive.
So nature's joys bring you delight,
the bay, the beach suit you just right.

10. BLUE HERONS

If you have seen blue herons fly,
    you've seen their very wide wingspan.
Their beauty's sure to catch your eye;
    you'll wonder at creation's plan,

a plan that brings to life each bird
    with many diff'rent habitats,
and species of which you've not heard,
    and some with plumes that look like hats.

The herons of the color blue
    with wingspans almost three feet wide
display a beauty through and through,
    a beauty nature cannot hide.

Blue herons are so sleek in flight,
    their heads point forward, their feet back.
How elegant this heav'nly sight.
    O what a joy their flight to track.

11. In Africa

The Maasai Mara seen at dawn,
    at any time of year,
amazes you as you look on
    as animals appear.
Giraffes and zebras, wildebeests
    their annual trek begin,
while lions, lords of all the beasts
    are seen just now and then.

The zebra, wildebeest, gazelle
    all form a giant train
of animals that soon will swell
    till millions form the chain.
They cross the Serengeti wide
    and travel miles on miles.
Though nature is alone their guide,
    they face unending trials.

The many that survive the tests
    that face them day by day,
perhaps as history suggests:
    they find they're on their way
to make the trek another year;
    again try to survive.
With dangers always very near,
    will they remain alive?

The world of Africa's unique—
    its mountains, lakes, and plains.
Its cultures have their own mystique,
    their cities, their remains.
The languages and unique dress,
    the cultures and lifestyles,
the lands of Africa express
    its hopes, as well as trials.

12. AFRICA'S OFFERINGS

With sights and sounds of early morn
    the Maasai Mara awakes.
One senses life has been reborn,
    as sunlight the darkness breaks.
One hears a giant lion's roar,
a hippopotamus' loud snore.

The Serengeti's wide expanse
    with jackals, rhinos, gazelles,
a thrill you'll find with every glance,
    which casts mysterious spells
of images you won't forget,
an elephant's and lion's duet.

The swiftness of a cheetah's pace,
    giraffes' regal demeanor,
an antelope's rushed leaps of grace
    make an observer keener,
lest one should miss a passing view
of all Africa offers you.

13. THE TEXAS LONGHORN

The Texas longhorn is a breed
    of cattle that derives from Spain.
Today they fill a lasting need
    for many things, food in the main.

They have a many-colored coat,
    perhaps they're black, or brown, or red,
and something else worthy of note:
    their horns can have an eight-foot spread.

The longhorn meat is very lean
    quite similar to venison.
"Enjoy a steak, see what I mean?"
    perhaps said poet Tennyson.

14. A SQUIRREL

A squirrel's agility's supreme;
it seems it does not need to scheme
how it will spring from here to there.
It seems to leap to anywhere:
from tree limbs to a chimney top.
One asks, do squirrels ever stop?
As if life were on a trapeze,
they float through air with greatest ease.
Across a narrow fence they run;
the squirrels play till day is done.
One grasps a walnut's shell to crack
and breaks it open for a snack.
A squirrel never seems to rest,
except when settling in its nest.
Into its nest you cannot see,
since it's so high up in a tree!

15. LIFE AS A SQUIRREL

Sometimes I wish that life could be
as playful as the squirrels I see.
The way they bound from tree to tree
without restraint, they're so carefree.

And then reality creeps in:
I see their scavenging begin,
which they repeat without chagrin,
for without food they will grow thin.

Their lives are not then so carefree,
though that's the way they seem to be.
Some things aren't as they seem, you see.
But that's the way they seem to me.

16. AN ACORN

An acorn fell down from a tree.
It bounced upon a roof, struck me.
It struck me right upon my head,
but acorn strikes you need not dread,
for squirrels find them a delight;
they savor every acorn bite.

17. BROODING TIME

Last summer in my blue spruce tree
    a pair of doves shared times to brood
upon their eggs, as I could see.
    Their actions I most keenly viewed.

Their posture was to me quite strange:
    the female sat from east to west;
the male, however, made a change:
    sat west to east upon the nest.

I'm sure they knew just what to do,
    for all day long the male sat there,
but as the moon came into view,
    the female brooding time would share.

Within two weeks two chicks were born,
    but they were scarcely to be seen.
I heard them chirping one fine morn,
    and saw them, what a lovely scene!

18. BIRDSONG'S RETURN

So brightly streams the morning light
    that stars are quickly dimmed.
The sun removes the dark of night;
    horizons are blue trimmed.

Across the plains the sunlight creeps
    and skirts the mountain peaks.
The trees are filled with small birds' peeps
    that were not heard for weeks.

The snow and sleet kept them away,
    but now here comes the spring.
Come March, come April, and come May.
    Oh! How the birds do sing.

A symphony of birdsong's heard;
    there's scarcely a brief pause.
For birdsong no one needs a word;
    it's music without flaws.

19. BLUEBIRDS, SPARROWS, CHICKADEES

The morning air, how crisp, how fair,
and on my fence a bluebird pair
are preening one another there.

A sparrow, chickadee alight
but don't disturb the blue's delight,
and soon the chickadee takes flight.

The sparrow sits alone awhile,
quite undisturbed, has its own style;
yes, sparrows have their own profile.

They flitter here and flitter there,
they rarely stop their time to share;
they've very little time to spare.

But there one sits upon the fence;
I'm wondering will it fly hence?
But there it sits. Does that make sense?

Then with a flash of lightning's light
the bluebirds, sparrow all took flight.
That's right, not one was then in sight.

20. A MALLARD PAIR

A pair of mallard ducks return
    each year and grace my lawn.
It seems they for each other yearn
    and stay from dusk till dawn.

Perhaps they find their favorite food
    or fav'rite place to sleep,
perhaps a nest their eggs to brood
    and ducklings safely keep.

The drake's adorned with a green head
    and collar lily white.
The hen is streaked with brown instead,
    so she'll stay out of sight.

I'm glad each year when they come back.
    I know that soon there'll be
occasionally a gentle quack,
    and ducklings I may see.

21. LIKE CROWS

The crows are squawking on the street,
for they have found something to eat.
But who has rights to eat's unsure,
not one of them displays demur.
They squabble, make outrageous noise,
not one of them the feast enjoys.
My! My! People can act like crows,
and yet it seems this no one knows.

22. A MAGPIE'S VISIT

A magpie settled on my fence,
a bird that's said to have much sense.
It looked at me as if to say,
"Now how are you, my friend, today?"
He preened a bit, feathers black, white.
I must admit he seemed quite bright.
I've heard that magpies can play games,
that's one of many magpie claims.
Intelligent they're said to be
and work in teams, a sight to see.
I've heard magpies also can grieve,
but how can someone this perceive?
I love the most to hear them sing,
for every tone's a thrilling thing.

23. YOU TOO?

A mouse looks up at a giraffe,
a sight that sometimes makes me laugh.
An animal so tall, so small,
these broad extremes we need recall,
because each must survive somehow
in nature's realm of here and now.
This is creation's unique plan:
its creatures cover a wide span—
from condors' wingspan to a grouse,
from tall giraffes to a small mouse.
A lesson here for humans too?
Creation has a place for you!

24. CHIPMUNK 1

A chipmunk scampered to and fro;
where did the chipmunk want to go?
It scratched the ground hoping to find
some grain the birds had left behind.
It quickly jumped up on a tree
to see, of course, what it could see.
It grasped an acorn in its paws,
it was so big it had to pause.
The acorn dropped and with a crack,
it seemed the chipmunk had the knack
to get his day's most precious meal.
I wonder how it made him feel.

25. CHIPMUNK 2

The chipmunk crawled up a brick wall;
his sharp claws did not let him fall.
It looked like bird seed he might rob,
but that turned into a tough job.
With just one paw he tried and tried
to grab a bird feeder he spied.
He stretched and stretched and in a flash
the chipmunk came down with a crash!
So unsuccessful in his quest,
he sat down just to take a rest.
And then a sparrow saw the grain.
Thank goodness! Both could eat again.

26. WOODPECKERS

Woodpeckers are of many kinds,
    some dressed in colors black and white;
but others wear quite different signs:
    red heads, red bellies, what delight!

How similar's the noise they make:
    a constant, rhythmic pecking sound.
These unique birds can silence break,
    wherever woodpeckers are found.

When pecking loudly on a tree,
    try tapping out their rhythmic sound.
And if you do it rapidly,
    you'll find their rhythms quite profound!

27. HUMMINGBIRDS

A hummingbird can flap its wings
    first forwards, backwards, upside down.
They are attracted by red things,
    and shiny colors: red, green, brown.

But hummingbirds don't really hum;
    their flutt'ring wings make humming sounds.
A constant hum is the outcome,
    as flow'r to flow'r they make their rounds.

Five hundred miles non-stop some fly,
    perhaps three thousand miles their trip,
so high not captured by the eye,
    as if they're nature's own spaceship.

Their lifespan's no more than five years;
    their beauty is not bound by time.
Each time a hummingbird appears
    their own aesthetics are sublime!

28. THROUGH A WINDOW PANE

The wonder of a window pane,
through which I see sunshine and rain,
opens my eyes that I may see
the world outside with clarity.
The trickling water streams whose flow
sometimes are fast, sometimes are slow,
run down the window glass with ease,
in wiggling streaks that often please.
This morning through my window pane
I saw a rabbit once again;
with rapid pace it hurried by,
then stopped; I saw the reason why:
my succulent sweet peas in bloom
the rabbit quickly did consume.
Just then a chipmunk came in view;
I wondered then, what would it do?
It grabbed an acorn, ran away;
my window pane had made my day!

29. CROWS AND SHINY THINGS

When crows alight a snowbound place,
how often they will leave a trace.
One sees the tracks of their broad feet,
no evidence of a retreat.
An open bag of garbage lies
as evidence of many tries
to find something that they can eat,
or find something that is a treat,
or use to build a needed nest,
in which some newborn crows may rest.
A shining object one crow spied
and caught it in his beak to hide,
to hide it from the big crow band,
so they won't know what he had planned.
The center of a nice new nest
is where he thought it would be the best
to put it, and with twigs around,
the place to hide it had been found.
When you see crows out in the snow
here's something that you need to know:
don't drop a ring or shiny thing
that sparkles, or it may take wing,
and wind up in a big crow's nest
where it is destined long to rest!

Section 2
Magical Flowers and Trees

30. A ROSE

I counted petals of a rose
    and thought of all the ways
a rose is fortunate to pose,
    the many roles it plays.

A rose adorns a bride's bouquet,
    adorns an evening gown;
expresses love in its own way,
    lifts spirits when they're down.

Red roses may one's love express,
    without speaking a word,
in joy or in deepest distress,
    though not a word is heard.

Therein resides the rose's pow'r:
    it thrills one deep within,
or comforts in the bleakest hour:
    reminds where love has been.

31. A GIANT TULIP TREE

There was a giant tulip tree
    that stood in our front yard.
It was my favorite place to be
    when rain came down so hard.

The limbs were thick and leaves were full;
    I rarely felt the rain.
Under the tree was never dull,
    though thunder was a strain.

With thunder's first clap, mother called,
    "Come in now from the tree."
I hesitated and I stalled,
    but she knew best for me.

But when the sun came out, I ran
    to sit under *my* tree.
And my own world again began,
    a world arranged for me.

32. DESERT FLOWERS

As warm sun rays touch rain-drenched sand,
comes something wonderful and grand.
Then suddenly before one's eyes
appears an elegant surprise,
for desert flow'rs by moisture fed
make of the sand a flower bed.
Before the sand is dried of rain
the desert flow'rs appear again.
They've not been seen for two years past.
How long, one wonders, will they last?
O desert flow'rs, we long to see
you blooming much more frequently!

33. MUMS' DELIGHT

Just now some little blooms of mums
    burst forth in yellow bright.
They'll bloom outside till the cold comes;
    till then they're a delight.

Some mums have colors of red wine
    and others violet.
I look out at them when I dine,
    since winter's not here yet.

But soon I'll bring the mums inside,
    lest there should come a frost.
If not, I fear they will have died;
    that were a dreadful cost.

So I'll enjoy them while I can,
    and care for them each day,
extend perhaps the mums' life span,
    my own color bouquet.

34. MAUNA KEA'S SILVERSWORD

One afternoon I dared to spy
a plant that quickly caught my eye.
A barren, bleak volcanic slope
bore in a flower signs of hope,
that there, ev'n there, life could survive,
I saw the silversword alive.
Mauna Kea's silversword
cannot and must not be ignored.
Endangered now for many years,
its loss would be the cause for tears.
The conservation effort's strong
the silversword's life to prolong.
Its silver-pointed-foliage grace
on barren soil leaves beauty's trace.

35. THE HIBISCUS

The flower named hibiscus
    has quite a lovely name.
Though rhyming with meniscus,
    that's not its claim to fame.

Its fame lies in its beauty,
    both elegant and rare.
To praise it is no duty,
    what joy this flow'r to share!

Its blooms can be radiant pink
    but with a heart deep red.
Its pink face makes me bethink
    the beauty it will spread.

I love its round, happy face
    that welcomes all who pass.
Its colors add charm and grace
    like elegant stained glass.

36. THE EVERGREEN TREES

I love that evergreens endure,
    especially at Christmas time.
They have their own special allure,
    as Christmas trees in every clime.
An evergreen or spruce that's blue
    will give you holiday delight,
just like the Christmases you knew
    when Santa came, though out of sight.

Our evergreen this year is decked
    with dazzling strings of colored lights,
each one that my papa just checked,
    burned brightly through the winter nights,
the nights of Advent, Christmas too
    until Epiphany is through.
And when another year is new,
    I'll wish "Happy New Year to you."

37. A SURVIVING DAISY

I stepped outside into the cold
    and much to my surprise,
I never thought I would behold
    the sight before my eyes:
a pink-faced daisy had survived
    the terribly cold night.
How glad I was that it arrived
    before the first frostbite.

I thought it best to pluck the flower
    for just in a short while
its stem would droop, losing its power,
    also the daisy's smile.
I placed it in a long-stemmed vase
    on grandma's planter stand.
There I'll admire its lovely face,
    so glad it is at hand.

38. PINK DOGWOODS

Pink petals of a dogwood tree
    wave gently in the morning breeze.
Their wistful beauty artfully
    by nature's brush is formed with ease.

The sunlight playfully peeks through
    the branches as they're moved apart,
displaying an amazing view
    of nature's momentary art.

The petals flutter to and fro,
    as gentle wind gusts lend their touch.
It seems that nature may well know
    that I love pink dogwoods so much.

39. A SWEETGUM TREE

The saplings of a sweetgum tree
look nothing like what they will be.

So thin and scrawny with few limbs,
when they are grown, they'll flow'r like gems.

Their leaves will be like pointed stars;
their blooms all colored red like Mars.

Their leaves in fall may turn rich red;
as colors through a forest spread.

The sunlight gives the red a sheen,
a dazzling beauty to be seen.

I'd love to plant a sweetgum tree
so there'd be mornings I would see

a sweetgum tree when it's in bloom,
for which each year nature makes room.

40. A HYACINTH

I saw a hyacinth in blue,
unusual, a striking hue.
Its petals cradled morning dew.

They sparkled in the dawn's sunlight
like diamonds glist'ning ever bright;
O what a most intriguing sight!

Above the hyacinth a rose
stood silently in regal pose.
What fragrance from the rose arose!

I love the hyacinths in bloom;
for them all gardens should make room
to be a gardener's heirloom.

41. GIANT SEQUOIAS

Sequoias' regal posture soars
    above the heights of other trees.
In all the varied out-of-doors,
    there are no other trees like these.

Their width, their height, their colored bark
    of cinnamon rich-colored frame,
bring wonder to a National Park
    and to Yosemite's proud name.

Their branches rise up to the sky
    avoiding flames from forest fires.
Though fires have caused some trees to die,
    they're nature's own cathedral spires.

"Preserve these links to history's past,"
    should be a common goal today.
With care and nurture they will last;
    Sequoias thus won't fade away.

42. LANDSCAPES

The landscapes' contours fascinate,
and artists to them gravitate,
drawn by their undulating hills,
their valleys, rivers, winding rills;
a forest filled with giant trees
and shorelines that are trimmed by seas,
a desert lined with miles of sand,
and an oasis nature planned,
a mountain peak with roaming goats,
and golden fields of growing oats.
Where'er we look they have no end,
for landscapes round the world extend.

43. RED AND GREEN

My holly tree has berries green;
there are no red ones to be seen.
It's summer, I have no concern
that into red ones they will turn.
That's nature's way, it takes its time
in New York or in Anaheim.
Each continent shows nature's force
will grow its flora in due course.
There's such a widened color skein—
with red and green it's never plain.

Section 3
Magical Seasons

44. REALLY?

The temperatures are up and down;
    this morning it is sixty-two.
But yesterday I had to frown;
    at thirty what was I to do?

The fall and winter all-in-one
    is not the way that it should be.
In fall I don't want winter sun;
    in winter, please not eighty-three.

Has global warming turned this round,
    and we have summer in the fall,
and winter no more can be found,
    and spring will no more come at all?

45. FALL, COME AGAIN

Today the grass was filled with leaves;
    in autumn they come down.
A few were caught under the eaves;
    most all of those were brown.

But earlier this fall the skein
    of colors was divine;
their beauty how can one explain,
    all colors did combine.

The leaves of some oak trees looked red,
    but there were yellows too.
And maple trees preferred instead
    a multi-colored hue.

How magical is autumn time
    when green leaves entertain
and turn to colors so sublime,
    we say, "Fall, come again."

46. AUTUMN BEAUTY

I stepped into a quiet lane
    that autumn colors fill.
It seemed the leaves were all aflame
    from sunlight, what a thrill!

A maple tree's bright orange leaves
    were stunning to behold.
They change how one the world perceives,
    as if beauty controlled,

controlled our thoughts, our actions too,
    indeed how we behave,
for beauty transforms what we do
    till we such beauty crave.

All we need do is look around,
    for beauty's everywhere.
The richly colored leaves abound,
    a beauty all can share.

The colors of each autumn leaf
    are colors that inspire.
And though the beauty may be brief,
    such beauty I desire.

47. NATURE'S COLOR SKEIN

The leaves along my street are red,
as autumn colors start to spread.
At light of dawn they do not glow
the way they do in sunlight's flow.
As morning light slowly appears,
the dawn mist fades, and then it clears.
A Ginkgo tree stands all alone
and lends to red a different tone.
Its leaves turn to a softened gold,
a stunning image to behold.
The gold amid the color red,
is but a single color thread
among the nature color skein,
where many colors tend to reign.

48. LEAF LIFE

Most leaves are born for a season,
    which lasts from spring until fall,
when colors give them new reason
    each passerby to enthrall.
The gold, bright orange, brown, and red
weave such a glorious color thread.

The sunlight strikes the gold and red
    with glistening, sparkling streams
of bright reflections, gently spread,
    an art that is made of dreams.
The wonder of such natural art
is wonder that enthralls the heart.

49. FALL'S COLOR-SPREAD

A tree beside my house turns red,
as autumn colors start to spread.
Behind my house yellow's the theme
as sycamores in sunlight gleam.
But on a single maple tree
there's yellow, orange, red to see.
A post oak tree that's very old
has leaves that want to turn to gold.
But some trees are just evergreen,
the only color they have been.
I'm thankful for fall's color-spread;
I'd not prefer just one instead.

50. THE MAGIC OF SPRING

As if one waved a magic wand,
the springtime of which I am fond
bursts forth with colors, blooming flow'rs,
which I may gaze upon for hours.
Camellias, a gardenia bush,
both give my soul a springtime rush
of fragrance and a color skein,
delightful in sunshine and rain.
The earth is blessed with many-a hue
of colors, smells that life renew.
So, come again, dear springtime, come,
with you I always feel at home.

51. EARLY SPRING

Down in the woods a redbud tree
has bloomed for all around to see.
It's early spring, most trees are bare,
but thankfully the redbud's there.
And just behind a giant oak
a dogwood spreads its snow-white cloak.
So, red and white the woods adorn,
as springtime once again is born.

52. SPRING

The spring explosion of new flowers,
refreshing rain of April showers,
are nature's way to start again,
creation's long, enduring chain
of life from life that is reborn,
when life and death face a new morn.
What joy the changes seasons bring,
around the earth, it's not just spring.
One hemisphere has winter, fall,
another has no spring at all.
But bring on spring where it's alive,
for it's in springtime that I thrive.

53. SPRINGTIME HIGH

A fluff of white just smiled at me
    from blooms of an azalea bush.
Outside a springtime jamboree
    of flowers gives my soul a rush,
a rush of springtime colors, smells,
    of chirping birds and bright blue sky.
The love of spring within me swells;
    my spirit's at an all-time high.

54. COLORS OF SPRING

Pink dogwoods seem to have their way
to set the springtime into sway.
Their color fills a forest bare,
a color which at first is rare.
Then comes the green, comes dogwood white,
and redwood trees drink in sunlight.
While lilies rest upon a pond,
bluebonnet blooms are just beyond.
And lavender fills up a field:
the winter's barrenness is healed.

55. MONTANA SPRING?

Does there exist Montana spring
    when snowdrifts rise to eight feet high?
What weather will March, April bring
    to Bozeman or to the Big Sky?
In other climes azaleas bloom:
    in Texas a bluebonnet field
may thrive, but Bozeman has no room
    for flow'rs when spring's not yet revealed.

It's put off spring for a few weeks
    so that the frozen ground can thaw,
until a crocus through earth peeks
    and Easter lilies evoke awe.
It's then Montana blossoms forth
    and blooming flowers, trees are seen.
From deepest south to the far north,
    Montana's ready to turn green.

56. SPRING'S NEW LIFE

Outside the first azaleas bloom
    in lovely pink and white.
It's nature's moment spring to groom
    with colors soft and bright.

The dark, gray winter colors fade
    with hyacinth's bright blue,
and buttercups in light or shade
    have a rich yellow hue.

Camellias, tulips, peonies
    with fragrant blooms now burst,
and butterflies and honey bees
    in nectar are immersed.

Spring, spring, the time when earth renews,
    and life begins again,
inspires us a new life to choose,
    so life's not lived in vain.

57. IT'S MAY

It's May with green grass and green trees,
warm sun's brought winter to its knees.
The gardens burst with buds and blooms.
I've windows open in my rooms,
so I can see and I can smell
gardenias that I love so well.
Their fragrance is a special treat.
Does it reach neighbors down the street?
If so, that will give me a thrill,
the evidence of nature's skill:
what's shared with one is shared with all.
It's nature's constant curtain call.

58. THE IMPORTANCE OF GREEN

In summer your green leaves are seen,
    majestic sycamore,
but autumn soon will change the scene,
    as it has done before.

The miracle of nature turns;
    your green in time will change.
The colors each observer learns
    are never drab or plain.

How grateful, sycamore, you'll be
    when dressed in colors bright,
and yes, leaves once more green we'll see—
    no green, no fall delight!

59. CARRY ON

When summer comes, snow will be gone,
and summer flow'rs will carry on
with color changes, fragrances
across a range of distances
from Germany to Timbuktu,
the USA to Katmandu.
The blooms and colors fascinate
as they creation celebrate.
The blossom nectars orchestrate
a symphony so delicate
of butterflies and humming bees
our eyes, ears, noses all to please.
This is a time to idolize
with beauty right before our eyes.
When summer comes, we'll carry on
for autumn, winter, spring are gone.

60. SUMMERTIME

How swiftly passes summertime
when springs and brooks are in their prime.
The songbirds serenade at will
and brightly beams each daffodil,
for summer sun can cast a spell
upon the flowers I know well.
With lovely heather on the hill,
it seems that Mother Nature's skill
surpasses all that I might dream,
ev'n solace beckoned by a stream.
My thoughts are deepened by its flow,
so gentle, peaceful, and I know
no place provides such ecstasy,
such joy in nature's constancy.
So, summertime, come round each year;
I eagerly await your cheer.

61. "I MUST GO DOWN TO THE SEAS AGAIN."

I went to the beach again this summer;
I missed the warm sand all winter,
and the ocean spray upon my face.
The early morning sun's gentle caress
took away all thoughts of snow and ice.
The sprigs of tall grass on the dunes
reminded me of fertility beneath the sand.
I saw the birds I never see at home;
I live near woods without seagull nests.
The nights' cool breezes lulled me to sleep.
I waked reluctant on the day of departure.
Just one more glimpse of the waves,
then I'll know they'll be there next year.
To leave the sea and sand is never easy.
Like the mountains, they have a magnetism
that draws me back to them again and again.
Sea and sand have their own winsomeness.
So do magical sunsets and sounds of gentle,
rippling waves, or surging billows in a storm.
It's no surprise that a poet once said,
"I must go down to the seas again."[1]
Go there once, and you'll say this too.

---

1. This is a line from a poem by British poet John Masefield.

62. A WINTER FEELING

A winter feeling's in the air;
outside my window trees are bare,
and snow is falling everywhere.

A large grey squirrel scampers round,
but not an acorn's to be found,
and rarely does one hear a sound.

A cardinal's red coat seems bright
as it reflects the dawn's sunlight,
especially as it takes flight.

The children just across the street
are playing in the snow and sleet,
while taking time each one to greet.

And there are many passersby,
who see the children are not shy.
They quickly say, "Hello! Goodbye!"

63. WINTER WINDS

The winter winds now chill the air;
there is no question they are there.
I exhale and the air turns white;
I stand too long, and there's frostbite.
I never leave my gloves behind,
unless they are too hard to find.
If so, that's something I'll regret,
for frozen hands are a bad threat.
I step across the frozen grass,
the crunch sounds like some broken glass.
The winter wind will not let loose;
its grip is like a tightened noose.
But once it brings in winter snow,
the skis and sleds are set to go.
The children love the snow-filled land,
for winter fun makes a dreamland!

64. DELIGHTFUL CHILL

The morning chill fits me just right,
for it was very cold last night.
The morning air's filled with a chill;
I breathe, inhale, and my lungs fill.
The morning chills quickly recall
hot summer days before the fall.
Yes, I prefer fall's cooler air,
it's autumn's pleasant bill of fare,
which it delivers with delight
by sunlight or by calm moonlight.
The seasons, nature's gen'rous gift
from hillside flow'rs to a snowdrift,
are images I won't forget
and pleasant thoughts which they beget!

65. SO COLD

When winter's here, snow may appear;
my skin feels thin, when snow creeps in,
and when thin-skinned, winter's no friend.
One does not doubt, it's cold without.
One cracks the door, feels it the more.
If snow comes down all over town,
one stays inside from cold to hide.
When weather's dire, one builds a fire.
A street's black ice does not entice,
but rather makes you test your brakes.
Yet snow is fun with each sled run.
And children gleam with snow ice cream.
O summer, spring, come have your fling,
the winter cold makes me feel old.

66. GUESS WHAT?

The ice was frozen on the street,
so hard and slippery to my feet.
Along a slope I felt them slip;
my shoe soles seemed to have no grip.
At first I swayed just to my right;
my balance held with all my might.
I noticed I began to slide,
my anxiousness I could not hide.
So I called out, "Help, help, someone."
My upright stance I thought was done.
Just as I passed an old park bench,
a stretched-out hand ready to clench
my flailing arms, caught me in time:
an unexpected pantomime.

67. A SNOWY PATHWAY

The snowflakes gracefully align
along a pathway trimmed with pine.
On either side a large snowdrift
had giv'n the pathway a facelift.
The path was lined on both its sides
with gravel until it divides.
Right in the Y of the divide
there stood an oak tree four feet wide.
Beyond the oak tree snow was deep,
and there a young deer tried to leap
across the path without success
and now it was in deep distress.
I plodded and trudged through the snow
And as I did, I did not know
if I could help to set it free.
It stared at me with longing eyes.
As I reached forward, what surprise:
the young deer suddenly was freed
and my assistance did not need.
I turned and saw a snowy glade
where winter beauty was displayed.

www.ingramcontent.com/pod-product-compliance
Lightning Source LLC
Chambersburg PA
CBHW061501040426
42450CB00008B/1438